For Phyllida

Poems

by

Fabian

Peake

Akerman Daly   Ridinghouse

I
have
a
measure
of
impostor
syndrome
with
words.
I
link
my
poetry
firmly
with
painting...

Fabian Peake discusses his poems with Eileen Daly and Jeremy Akerman

Eileen Daly

There's a definite sense that you are writing poems to be looked at as well as heard. Tell us about the visual look of your poems?

Fabian Peake

The gaps and spaces between words and lines give a sense of time and changing circumstances. The poem's life is in my head as well as on the page. This might seem to be a contradiction, because many of the poems appear like concrete poems, but they do not employ the same methods or hard abstraction of concrete poetry. I use the gaps and spaces as ways of distancing myself from a phrase or idea that might have just occurred; they are like separate thoughts.

Jeremy Akerman

An underlying theme in all the poems is delight in observation mixed with feelings of loss. Another combination is surprise and disquiet, 'a shock-wave wind blew open the doors of reason' for instance from *Fungi*. Many poems have a quiet anger that, although gently put, is persistent; 'he is annoyed, I am annoyed', comes to mind from *it took time for the green*. I read these undercurrents as you coming to terms with life. Is that their function for you?

FP

I work with veils when I'm writing. My relationship with writing is complex because as well as getting in touch with realities of emotion, I also want to skirt round certain subjects. Often, I experience half-formed ideas or ideas which elude me, and find myself stabbing about to unearth a thought or phrase of which I can feel fully convinced. The emotional element in the poems is restrained. I am suspicious of it, as I want to avoid clichés. I'd like to write 'I love you', but in a surprising way. Yes, I think the poems are angry at times.

ED

Are poems like *song thrush* written to be spoken aloud? Is there a difference between writing for the page and for the ear?

FP

The poem *song thrush* was built round the idea of listening to a song thrush singing in the park across the railway tracks from where I live. I wanted to know what the bird might be saying if I was able to understand it. The song thrush repeats phrases four or five times before inventing another melodious utterance. To answer the question, I would say yes, there is a huge difference. *Mistake*, for example, uses repetition and spatial gaps – the timing of a poem changes radically when read aloud as opposed to reading to oneself.

ED

You've written poems using fixed poetic forms, such as sonnets and villanelles, as well as writing in verse. Is using these established forms part of an experimentation process or something for you to push against or push towards?

FP

When I realised that poetry was becoming a force in my life, I decided to confront the question of poetic form. I have a natural discomfort with prescribed forms yet I acknowledged that they are a major part of poetry. I enrolled on many courses, learning about existing forms and putting them into practice. Writing sonnets, villanelles, terze rime etc., was a way of accumulating knowledge about the nuts and bolts of poetry. I felt imprisoned by those forms.

JA

Do you think words have fixed meanings or is meaning a changeable thing for you? How concerned are you to arrive at meaning?

FP

I think that words are highly changeable in their meaning, but of course it depends what words are used. Some words don't have much capacity for change while others are like chameleons. Some words feel really good but I might abandon them because they are promoted by vanity. I am led by my intuitions and am often surprised by the words or phrases that are vomited up. Re-reading my own poetry is always surprising. Sometimes there is an unfamiliarity about the things that I have written and with that comes a sense of displacement that is unnerving. I am eager to arrive at a meaning but not one that is necessarily logical.

ED

Some of the poems, such as *stretched out over many miles* have a logical system to the way they are laid out on the page. Can you say how you write these 'abstract' poems?

FP

With these kinds of poems I have a more fixed idea before I begin. Some, for instance, take the first and last words of the lines of another poem. They are simply written down with no attempt to edit. The words themselves, though, are bound by their origins and the rule is, no changes. In other words, there is a system. In *stretched out over many miles* there was a simple idea of a one-word movement from top to bottom using an almost automatic writing method. A big part of some of these poems is the trust that I must have in my intuitions – I have to make the decision about keeping or jettisoning words or phrases that might have surfaced so violently from my mind.

Is what you can do with words more risky than what you can do with images. Are words more dangerous?

Perhaps. I try to be equally 'dangerous' with images, but making pictures is my first profession and words were a later development. It's easier to be dangerous with a second profession. I have a measure of impostor syndrome with words. I link my poetry firmly with painting and feel slightly remote from the literary world. Many artists now work in different media but 40 years ago it was frowned upon.

You describe yourself as a painter who writes. Have you read the poems of other painter-poets, such as Hans Arp, Kurt Schwitters and Paul Klee? Can you describe your poems as written collages?

I think of my poems as paintings more than I think of my paintings as poems. The poems grow out of a visual background rather than from a literary one. I put the poems together in a similar way to the way a painting comes about. The thinking is the same. The construction is by means of collage (not literally but metaphorically). The poems move about on the page when I am writing them. The words and images change places with each other or are scrubbed out and abandoned along the way. A painted figure or abstract motif might be flung into the dustbin only to jump out again and re-instate itself.

Yes, I love the poetry of Arp, Schwitters and Klee. Visual artists write in a different way. There's something inexplicable about their approach to writing; it doesn't seem to come from the literary canon. This may or may not be true.

What poetry inspired you?

For many years I have been more inspired by poetry from outside the British Isles. Something closes up, for me, when I think of all the famous writers from Britain. American and European poets are my kindred spirits. Their thinking is completely understandable to me. Among the American poets that I have been influenced by are Wallace Stevens, William Carlos Williams, E. E. Cummings, Robert Creeley, Charles Olson, Robert Lowell and from Europe, Mallarmé, Dada poetry, Picabia, Pessoa and Georg Trakl.

LOOSE MONK

I'm talking about oranges rolling
between hedges, the flank of a lorry.
I'm talking about the Canadas, facing south
and remember the chevron of snow geese
waving like cotton high over South Side.

Home now, the fields have returned
to normal, their informal layout familiar
after the prone rectangles of America.
I'm talking about him being good for me,
showing me the open door, where before

in the middle of nowhere I drank
tea without thought. I'm talking about
the pullovered man, walking not talking
behind the screen of autumn. He nears
the shed, offloading its cladding.

I picture him striding through
rhymes and accents which elude me.
It's a short walk, but he stops where
I tell him. I'm talking about tongues
which stand in support, yet say nothing.

OUR HEDGE

The privet, the only living thing
in my line of fire, shivers
in a cool January blow, rustles
and stage whispers to others
in case they are there. Our hedge
is one of the last in the street;
most got grubbed up to make way
for the ending of hawk-moths.

SUNRISE

It crossed my mind
      (if minds can be crossed),
that the sky was on fire,
      (if skies can lose their tempers
and flame up like that).
      She looks at it and tells me
it's asayake in her language.
      I say it's sunrise burning, in mine.
The heating engineer is due
      at my house to mend a valve.
The valves in the sky, God's castle,
      are blown to pieces.

song thrush
song thrush

all I can say is that I want

                                            (to make them)
                                            (your cat has the meissen sign)

all I can say
all I can say is that I   (to make them)

he stands on the bobble   (a page, you know, of stylised shadows)
stands on the bobble. he stands

he stood, to change tense
I want to make them. I   (he no longer grasps the palette)
thrips is singular   (the definition)
he swallows a library
smoke. he swallows   (hirundine)
is that I want to make

                              (dropped, by chance, the digit fell akimbo)
to make them. to
make them. to make   (other traffic)

they've cleared the table; not a scrap   (left)
they've cleared the formica table
the blue formica   (it's always been there)

they've cleared the table;   (not a scrap)
not a scrap left; a scrap
not (they shiver ....)   (their wings)
they shiver. not a scrap

to make them
to make them   (distance)
to make .....   (others, putting their oars in)

but I'm waiting for a red nape
for a red nape. red. nape.   (head bobbed on the mesh)
there's one back from the dead

seen it in the swamps
seen it. seen it in the swamps.

there's one   (back from the dead)
there's the square type

the square type, square type
square type, the square type   (just look, that's all, at the pocket)

there's nothing to suggest   that while looking in the mirror   the books

shouldn't read backwards   get a book off the shelf and see   I can't

see round the corner   that you see round

down with equipment   to catch fish   if the fisherman   weighed

what then?   and what of swifts   was to do what he does   backwards

than anyone else's?   winter muscles in quickly now   slicing through summers   shorter

scribbling bushes   but where is the princess?   with its dense

it's as though reproducing   is a pleasure   she's hard to get to   to be accommodated   rather

than indulged   getting back to africa   is what hirundines want   its leaves

don't fall to ground   the laurel   but wreathe stone heads   in spanking

new museums   recently built recently seen   when all the others   having

disrobed   for the coldest part of year   why they should freeze   and sporting 'because I'm worth it'   wigs

stand wondering   it's a question of location   nothing

more   the hill in the window was your head   the tree's shadow spat yellow

at autumn   and her hair moulted   at the summit of a scottish summer

stretched
out
over
many
miles
the
gross
monster
orange-pink
body
(mauve
and
blue
in
the
shadows)
not
the
pinky-orange
boy
of
forties
london
came
apart
at
the
edges
fraying
into
evening
azure
and
joining
the
craneflies
the
bats
threatened
the
cousin
of
dusk

that light, the light of five
the light between dark and light
when autumn wrinkles to winter,
when clocks are forgotten –
some just octagonal fancies
for an artist's glance
when red turns to green;
that light clothes all things
in the wet birth of dawn –
books, the walls, painted treasures,
all stitched by the same needle.
a man's raised hand
loose and languid, is just
as chocolate as the hangered jacket,
just as mongrel as plato
or enid blyton. everything
is absent; everything is present.
look at the beard
on the big oak table. in that light
there's no beard, no diary,
no vinegar, no slash in the torso's side.
and colour? what colour?
scarlet breeches are merely
grey soup, like the wardrobe
in the corner – scotch broth,
brown windsor, mulligatawny.
dawn vaults over the mirror
and the blankets and walls
mumble in french.

THE SEARCH

I'm looking for you in the trees behind
the mist, unsure of who you are, but I have
your swirling, shot-silk patterns in my sights.

I'm looking in the night around the windows,
the brushed-on windows, wet into wet, line
across smear, and I only just believe.

I'm looking for you in the plum-tinted grey
of there; you do not mean to cheat or play
games – I expect and want you to hide.

The wind exhales through the waiting noon
and something's in the air – before its wordless
swoop I feel the stripes of the sparrowhawk.

And as I catch up on your mood half buried
in melancholy, I call you softly, glimpsing
your profile shadowed on the redshank marshes.

I'm looking where I think you'll never be,
behind the warp and weft, the other side
of invention, where you lie in wait for me.

The bucket I hold is empty,
all the policemen cast out.
I will wait a while and listen
to the rhythm of the trains –
and the music of the blackcap.

The day starts here
at the hole dug in the sand.
I want to know why
the Atlantic can't fit into it,
a bucket at a time.

Alone, my head lies on the oak table,
stories and dances stopped in their tracks.
My mouth gapes – the police are prone
on the deep pile carpet.
I lie down to play.

I change places. Outside the window
I am watching the bucket and I watch
my head. Which will fill first?
The brick wall ahead stands firm.
I press my back on its resolve.

THE LETTER

In the south ward she wrote her pleading letter
like columns of smoke on the thin, yellowed paper;
plumed signals of hope entreating him to get her
out of there. She didn't know he planned to escape her.

Her hand traced out only one pencilled word –
'Come, come ...' she spelt again and again,
laying each plea with care, like a nesting bird,
on the high branches and delicate twigs of her brain.

Did he return, to walk her in the troubled garden
and re-plant her missing language with a kiss?
Or did he seal his ears against her calls?

For without him there, her arteries would harden
and her vacant prayer vaporise with a hiss.
There will be no answer from those asylum walls.

THE WOMEN LOOK

At first, a quivering. There is no 'before time'.
There's always a place to name.
Seemingly static, everything moves. Cosmic walls
bear witness. The dust speaks before we hear it and
grit grows in the head. (The women look)
They are the same women; it is only the slant
of the sun that casts their shadows.

>   The car pulls in. Men polish its curving lines.
>   Blue body. He cried, the mechanic, when
>   the Delage swanned into his eyes. Forgotten
>   in a fairy tale, he found it in his memory.
>   Brushing off the grime, three brothers
>   fought over that car. The mechanic
>   turned the page. Boom, boom.

Whilst shaving, Father O'Shea missed some bristle
in the crease of his nose. Now, every morning when he shaves,
the artist remembers the priest - the grammarian.
Lift. (The women look). Perhaps there is an answer
behind the vapour. Iridescent beetles roll dung balls
in the artist's brain - the shining car; the cluster of bristles;
a single golden hair. The wind winds up.

>   The men and women are on the mountainside.
>   There's talk of group marriages.
>   Were the never-visited communes
>   of his younger days, imitating?
>   A choice - one man, many wives.
>   Or: nine women, nine men, one team, procreating.
>   Australia. (The women look)

Squinnying, the oracle guides a thought
down the wormhole of uncertainty, willing himself
to see round corners. He sees cul-de-sacs
encircled by rubber heads.
A curtain twitches. 'Don't look; you will be punished.'
The penalty - two severed fingers.
Crescendo. A skeleton is born.

The cul-de-sac is quiet. Tall as men, the heads ruminate.
Further off, stone faces parade single file
on a path of blind approval. They must not look.
Slowly, the rubber heads swivel on plinths, thoughts
snagging on the brambles of their minds.
'Don't touch. Don't touch.' (The women look)
Gossips in the new town flex itchy fingers.

Winding down to Cromwell; his grandfather's middle name.
Straw hair, matted across the writer's crown, conceals
royal schemes below her skull. Gleaned from reality,
the sorcerer cannot stomach the tale. 'Don't write like that!
You will spend six years in the wilderness.' (The women look)
So, the pen is on the throne, alone on a velvet cushion.
'Don't tell me about your cousin or your best friend's mother!'

We are in the rooms. The rooms house the
special ones. The mechanic brought the Delage
to the red room. It stood in the painting, wheels
at rest on a leopard skin. He cries for the bonnet – the long lines,
the smooth surface, the curving blue beauty.
He drops to his knees before the grille, lauding
the might of the car, his god.

She let him in. Crossing the Atlantic took her home.
Cockroaches are the inevitable outcome
of bleeding eyes at Darlington station, its circular windows
inviting flux and the mastery of a drilling imagination.
The vacuum freezes, chisels its shoulders, finds its tongue.
Backbone. I have the whale's vertebra. I know the story
and from where the bone was cleaved. I have it to worship.

No myth. The artist's father cut out the vertebrae
on the beach. Three grey bones dwell in the houses
of his children and stand as riddles for visiting quizzers.
One bone got requisitioned for the ending of missionaries
when mongooses scented the sunsnakes. (The women look)
Still standing in water, the plane tree points to the book.
We have come to the gate and the wind is dead.

THE LOOTER

I lifted the lid on a thought,
a smell came out. Rebellion

raged in Hankow when the world
was black and white.

He turned the corner of a street;
a charred telegraph pole

exclaimed its brand of justice –
nailed up by the pigtail, a head;

cheap umbrellas and skeins
of wool hung alongside.

Doc hid down wells,
fled into cornfields,

knotted sheets, packed the piano
for safe return to England.

There, the shopkeeper
weighed apples on the counter.

HE WALKS THE HORIZONTAL LADDER

it speaks quietly
below the umbers and rusts.

he climbs now to the path
we call the sandy one.

will he be taken to a place
of certainty (a cast-iron plate

in the mud) where
he will loosen his tongue?

back in the lake the pike
waits for the ice to crumble,

but here, the sun draws its black lines
on the slope where another story sprawls

and he alerts himself
to green sounds, green smells.

inside the woollen days he is elsewhere,
not listening, not smelling the clouds.

yet his eyes are his tongue.

he will swim, one day,
across the desert

and stand upright on the rungs.

YET

yet
before
the fan of mud
anyway
speed of growing grass is comparable
was a pile today of orange (a beautiful orange
you know, the kind with a dash of vermilion)
plastic pipes
before I checked
I called it a garganey
gadwall
was the one
vermiculations always make me fall in love
of course, otherwise
along the rails I'm stopping here
lyhedra with three-point frequency
the red car is gone
yet
yet
will we see a roadrunner?
the unknown, the desert
voices, voices
well no, he came to us
where there was once a warehouse
om wastegro
all those twigs, a wig, peering over the straight
hastening away
ho wants to under
yet

WOODCOCK

I say it flew over London making for another
          green place   a place to hide its bill
wood   park   forest   chase

I had never seen one   I had never seen a woodcock
          but   I knew it when I saw it dead
          the stripes   running crossways on its head
I knew it from the books   and   the butcher's
 the books: flat colour plate   the butcher's: warm breast squeezed

the species of death a riddle
no blood on the plate glass   it lay still on concrete
          wing feathers lifted   by the wind   (like he said about his verbs
          and sheet rubber)

but
how, how, how   and   when, when, when

          she guessed, it hit a pane above   and
          plummeted   to modern earth   long straight bill
still pointing   long bill killed by   the invisible glass

I am the man of leaves   look in the black window

it got bagged up   nobody wept   we stared
a week later, another crashed the tower
               not flushed   but   stopped in air

don't come near me   wild is wild

          and the eyes   inside the saucer
          and the eyes
          and the eyes   glass
          and the eyes

haloes   like pressed flowers   held their own   in the thin
     publication   likewise the words (las palabras)

I say it flew over London

29

this alley a brick wall
this from or is a
plume out I noticed steam
opposite out of the wall –
smoke the my of itself
is about opposite have smoke
breathed out of this suppose
from the wall itself something
and the alley opposite alley
heating out of the wall
the smoke house plumed exhaled
smoke of house plume a
a plume of smoke but
really wall the plumed smoke
of the the out smoke
the smoke of steam of
about noticed and smoke out
the plumed of really the
wall the exhale brick but
house itself alley I've looking
exhaled the smoke from out
this this plume opposite smoke
is breathed from and heating
the smoke a really of
the about the wall house
exhaled it plume exhaled smoke
is house alley from out
out the about out the
the out smoke of plume
it smoke of wall the
plume not is the wall
exhaled a plume alley of
smoke out of itself that
is that smoke like the
house is smoking opposite really

TWO STEP

jobless + extend + welfare + produce +
something + budget + rather + Jesus +
seeing + stages + recent + vision +
the roof tiles covered in snow? no,
it was a violet light. doubting +
worship + subside + hillock + enough +
image + chancel + payment + German +
living + remains + rifle + jacket +
Cajun + you, Americans, have your
north-east shores; yachts, pilgrim fathers,
stores' lists. bomber + technique + slipshod +
flintlock + parson + kidneys + Castro +
Bogart + spider + maxim + milkman +
boatswain + between now and the end
of the year, the diary is more or less
blank. website + sinew + wineskin + perhaps +
moment + succour + seeming + taller +
snowdrop + keening + moles must be very
abundant, judging by all those hills, or
is there just one responsible? subject +
matter + pigskin + backfire =

All the barbers are brothers.
All the brothers are barbers.
You think it's him, but it's you.   You are a bottle, a spinney, a Wagler's pit viper.
                                      It's raining in the shape, much like the extract.
                                      Paint pulled the weather from his story.

delta. Fields; dog now Vex
dog Vex mount. fields pleasant
dogvex pleasant; bracket of sunshine
                    that. leaned on the privet
                    of blossom; Concrete uncertainty Of,
                    envelopes. envelopes Cornered hedge the
dogVex bracket. Of; sunshine pewter (   )
fields the; vexDog delta And –
hedge the cornered. Sunlight Bracket –
                    a bracket of sunlight leaned
                    on the privet   cornered the hedge
                    teacups for ears   no not in the window
It changes, all the way up,
all the way up – the yellow pole.
Inside, it would be a different story;
                    horns, you know, an' all.
                    Like the devil. What is he like?
                    He is you; the white beard says so.
Scribbles try, scribbles fail;
many eyes; tongues strain out;
rings for hands; duck's feet.
                    Ties slip sideways, only in line
                    and in the drawers, sex at the ready.
                    Bushes are not always easy.
All the drawers, gloss or walnut
hang out, empty now; empty of him,
his shaking foot stilled
                    Are you in that lonely shoe?
                    Are you in the haven of her thought?
                    Or in the silver toy zooming north, trundling south?
I should steel myself to be him,
for if I believe the man of iron
(and I don't), I have a million faces.

FRUITS

It's in the family, he said,
my little brother had one
when he was sixteen. I had
an apple-sized one working
itself round my body and now
I'm on rat poison every day,
ha ha! That's right, ha ha!

Listening to the man on the train
I thought of you, pregnant with
our second. They told you
yours was grapefruit-sized,
but they cut it out months before
she arrived, cherry pink.

AWAY IN TEXAS

Are those the monarchs, tilting angle-winged
between skyscrapers? I hold my hands in imitation.
'Where?' he says, 'I've seen none.'

But they are there in thousands, a few at a time,
the sun spitting orange through stained-glass veins.

I keep seeing Medina; Ephraim, I think.
He's upside down today, still smiling
in his Korean War army cap. Twice

since I've been here he's died – right way up
both times. I don't want the others, only Medina.

And all I can see of Shuckey Duckey
is the glitter of his golden jacket in the dark;
he's upside down too, yet from this angle

I could swear he's a dummy. I'll ask our friend
the photographer; she took the picture.

How come I don't know this Howdy Doody?
Y'all dropped his name on the concrete,
oblivious to the way letters scatter. Something

to do with early kids' TV (what does it matter?) –
a kind of Archie Andrews with teeth.

We all made an evening of red hair and freckles.
By sundown the big room had swallowed the dead,
the comedians and the cardboard streets.

I carried the fisherman across the floor
and laid it, gun drawn, by the door.

BLACK WINDS

The black winds collide
        with the black winds
Others, behind and green
        blow slower
Here and there a hand
        writes an explanation
in coloured words
        Am I above this commotion
or brazen?
        The pink ships
(tankers, freighters)
        set my viewpoint as a bird's eye
But literal is not the truth
        I have entered one room only
not the room chosen at birth
        That one was for Mexico

amalgammaglamaamalgammaglamaamalgammaglamaamalgamaamalgam
amalgammaglamaamalgammaglamaamalgammaglamaamalgamaamalgam
amalgammaglamaamalgammaglamaamalgammaglamaamalgamaamalgam
amalgammaglamaamalgammaglamaamalgammaglamaamalgamaamalgam
amalgammaglamaamalgammaglamaamalgammaglamaamalgamaamalgam
amalgammaglamaamalgammaglamaamalgammaglamaamalgamaamalgam
amalgammaglamaamalgammaglamaamalgammaglamaamalgamaamalgam
amalgammaglamaamalgammaglamaamalgammaglamaamalgamaamalgam
amalgammaglamaamalgammaglamaamalgammaglamaamalgamaamalgam
amalgammaglamaamalgammaglamaamalgammaglamaamalgamaamalgam
amalgammaglamaamalgammaglamaamalgammaglamaamalgamaamalgam
amalgammaglamaamalgammaglamaamalgammaglamaamalgamaamalgam
amalgammaglamaamalgammaglamaamalgammaglamaamalgamaamalgam
amalgammaglamaamalgammaglamaamalgammaglamaamalgamaamalgam
amalgammaglamaamalgammaglamaamalgammaglamaamalgamaamalgam
amalgammaglamaamalgammaglamaamalgammaglamaamalgamaamalgam
amalgammaglamaamalgammaglamaamalgammaglamaamalgamaamalgam
amalgammaglamaamalgammaglamaamalgammaglamaamalgamaamalgam
amalgammaglamaamalgammaglamaamalgammaglamaamalgamaamalgam
amalgammaglamaamalgammaglamaamalgammaglamaamalgamaamalgam
amalgammaglamaamalgammaglamaamalgammaglamaamalgamaamalgam
amalgammaglamaamalgammaglamaamalgammaglamaamalgamaamalgam
amalgammaglamaamalgammaglamaamalgammaglamaamalgamaamalgam
amalgammaglamaamalgammaglamaamalgammaglamaamalgamaamalgam
amalgammaglamaamalgammaglamaamalgammaglamaamalgamaamalgam
amalgammaglamaamalgammaglamaamalgammaglamaamalgamaamalgam

36

maglamaamalgammaglama maglamaamalgammaglama

EYE

I stand on the riverbank
attempting to understand.

Unseen, my eye scans the landscape.

The drawing is on the wall,
others are stored in the vault.

I look at the drawing,
I look at him drawing.

He draws the girl; I
watch him draw her.

I am not in the camp. I'm at the river.

Does she see him
looking at her?

The girl's head is flung back,
mouth gaping –

her rigid arms are dying, her
small chest rattling.

On the pillow her goodbye is imminent.

He asks 'Should I draw?'
I watch him falter. But

he continues. He
has been ordered there.

The girl's feather-light head coughs
and I fall in the river.

FOX (AUTO-DA-FÉ)

this is how it is this
side of the velvet curtain

        I didn't ask him that –
        nothing is known of the blind eye
        and the chicken pox

I wasn't told this is how it is
the curtains are heavy   cannot
be drawn   there's no gap
only skin only hide

        someone broke the night
        it was not the fox

never did he wear
two ties; he did today

        a cleaver shows a golden light
        curtains are the only night

and the long thin man
lay on the soft burglar
she will net his whole catch of books –
the Japanese and the Greek

        the men are all looking – she'll drape
        her starched blue skirt over the chair

he did today (if only the will!)
the books'll speak; the books'll
turn their backs   leaning in they'll
be dumb   and there'll be no dog on the ledge

    the thin man eats the pellets
      yearning for a better life
    all the rooms will be lost to another mind
    the other four a miscalculation

        there are boxes   but he did today
        and drawers   it's not here
        the name eludes me   something tax

he put two ties under his collar
pink pin-up (not a windsor,
definitely not monsieur!)

        perspectives are surprising when blue

HAMPSTEAD HEATH

Tense,
          on a tight summer evening,
       we walked on the hard track
                overhung with filigreed chords.
Playing the changes, the sun
          pinned petals of light
                on the grey beech trunks.
We came out into a pink waving meadow
          where caravans of picnickers
                trailed through grasses
                to an imminent concert;
          Tchaikovsky, someone said.
We turned
          and made a deep harbour
       in the bracken.

FUNGI

The sun burnt a hole in the sky
the day you took me mushrooming.
Our talk rifled through the copse,
voices ricocheting off silver bark.

Rain, sun, downpour, sparkle.
Squelching in mud we searched under
the corpses of beech trees fallen
in the Great Blow. You knew where to look

and probed with expert fingers.
We found a few – mainly Amanitas
like Grisette and its tawny cousin.
Beneath winking leaf cover we listened

to the distance droning like a hive.
Death Cap and Destroying Angel blunt-
nosed through soft ground at our feet.
You said the clouds were so beautiful.

Billowing, a porcelain-white mood
enveloped us and a shock-wave wind
blew open the doors of reason. You fell out,
plummeting to madness.

it took time for the green
fur coat to line my back.

I'd been lying there years
on the umber mud

since their decision;
freshly beached where

no water flowed
no breakers crashed.

they lay me down,
my skin a rhinoceros.

often he walked past
hurling dead sticks

for the black creature.
his eyes searched in my

bark for questions.
the green clothes of a decade

harboured not birds, not ticks,
but songs.

he is annoyed,
I am annoyed,

by that anti-camber.
the walk to my spot

tested his knees, his ankles –
yet he can go home.

I strain
at the brink of a slope.

APPROXIMATE (2)

... I've tried to write about you
and the pirates ..... we are twenty
minutes late .... that's a book
I wouldn't read ... still looking
... it's the way to do it, be bold ....
all the oils, sesame, olive .... dried
pigs' ears bagged in plastic ...
see her hands holding the red book
... he makes a tank stop in its tracks
after a tango shuffle ..... they go salsa
my daughters ... a great crack, stop,
look, nothing .... could've been ....
but the embankment sloped to
vast open fields ..... perhaps vandals
... scuba trip to the red sea, red
with blood ... still smoking? I
thought you'd .... we went again
to the vaulted jazz room ... it
can be done by a cockroach, just
pick up a stick ... or pick up
a skewer ..... draw a line in toast dust
.... or scrapings .... what can we
expect to see in the desert? ... furrows
in his forehead below the silver
sunrise ... riches of thought
interrupted by the edge of the page
... I never liked him .....

HIATUS

..... would of course be ... so ...
... realised that Gillian's ancestor .....
... some sort of fight .... narrow gulch ...
anyway ... in the river ..... news ...
... it got, or did it reach .... when
she said it, it didn't sink in ... the
library ... makes history in the twinkling
.... not a bat's wing .... could be ....
..... or ... and yet ... there were
others in that book whom I'm sure ....
he wouldn't have seen real Sumatran
fish until ... making history
was his forte .... better to go and judge
gaps ..... their antennae are so silted ...
... he can write what he likes ..... so ...
all over the floor, the work .... grumpy
faces ..... impossible to find the books ...
and his I never ... many times I've tried ...
.... big rivers are common in stories ....
... those ..... hadn't known ... they
died together ....

I say frigate – that's enough

    our ginger cat charlie
    met boutros boutros-ghali

these are uncemented bricks
not the flow of an ice-cold brook
in yorkshire

    we pass pylons
    criss-cross members jumbling
    my clear view

bricks bricks
bricks bricks
bricks bricks

in the next field
a horse wears his blanket
although it's summer
your horse has concrete hooves
I've named him rocinante

oak? ash?
they slip down the hill

the whole vista was middle green
until the cooling towers sprouted
a column of shocked smoke
which fused into cloud
no wind ruffled the shark-grey heavens

look at the size of the air booming
between sky and golf course

bricks bricks bricks
bricks bricks bricks
bricks bricks bricks

NOT AS IF

It wasn't as if,
for all we knew, the light,
the light gushed in
the big square window;
and for all we knew,
it wasn't as if the row
of low candlesticks
were flooded with the hour
before we rose. It wasn't
as if, for all we knew,
the morning's wet filled
full the lungs of slabs
lying ordinary and matter-
of-fact on the pavement.
It wasn't, it wasn't as if
the levellers hadn't been
put in the glass ashtray
whose use now is different.
And no one can say
it wasn't as if the cliff
of the day ahead soared
above the moment before
her arrival, but that we were
only, for all we knew,
waiting for something to happen.

MISTAKE

                    the mistake was in the sky
my hand
          bathroom window   back the
filthy as a thought
                        the moon burns before the cloud
        my hand
                          flicks   back the
tablecloth   ersatz curtain
                ersatz moon   a mistake
                                          mistake   back the
        the mistake was in the sky
the sun
the sun   invades   (is)
it's dark
                          in   (they'll be too)   near
            sleeping   my garden
in the corner   light bulb light bulb   we approach
        a probe goes there
                              three suns of heat   we burn
                          the tan   the mistake
        weeps from   her   her   her
            the mistake was in the sky
weeps from   trapped
shoulders those   pretty things   broken
        I water the sun   falls
                                          to
                brown   tablecloth
        join the pigeon
        I will know another time   wing   back the

49

all come find two is
I by most things mental
can or intriguing phenomena behind
say perhaps how if the
is it do you tree
that is you will there
I something tackle are lurks
have that those in a
an does passages? the presence
idea not I field which
about present have of holds
a insuperable invented vision knowledge
state problems a of but
of for story the secretes
in-between me about viewer this
I they a dreamer knowledge

mean come tree narrator it

something to (I'm writer will

very me always me not

particular quite bringing one divulge

but readily trees largely the

which anyway into straight methods

is it my ahead by

difficult is writing the which

to the and other one

define writing giving off can

it between them on interestingly

involves the human on verbalise

the things characteristics the one's

wording or or right mental

or objects at of ramblings

articulation or least the just

of as symbolic field ramble

thoughts I overtones) of I

on said and vision can

either images a I hear

side (do golden suppose you

of you tower the say

images know glittering substance but

images the in of it's

are imagists?) the this not

easy that unsunlight aforesaid that

to I these picture easy

they talk about colours   slow
magenta there, is there   d
                                   when there are none
theirs is in small flat
                         i   or blow softly
     two   it's not the same   ys in a word
         sound as spoon tick love   t   h
or tone   or tone
          boxes gut   their colour stays
         they just press their fingers
     the other colour, my colour, is colour   y

their colour, not being there, is more   mysterious
could you go and fetch my pen

                    if I touched colour   b
                    they reach hearts
                    or plucked tone   out of bridged   r

          not the dog food the rhythm
          when   pressing   the valve
     u
(lamb)   crossed out   a   a different emotion
listen, then   cheddar crossed out   bang on the dot
          he, of the organ and the birdsong
do not see   apostrophe   o   k   in   g

          m   washing up liquid   t
                       tomatoes   crossed out
          it's not (lamb)
salad   i   with a y between
dog biscuits   tectonic plates
rice   t'
iambs   all crossed out   squeeze dramas
s   in matter grey
          o   early dark in the   (fish cakes)
b   n
     no, to then   they   note   dinner plates
          number plates   misplaced
just   appears   have juice
or   or   bonnet   l
to   equate   tongue   room

                    52

they feel what they   (..............)   because

       dog   they're not in this   he

   blow   (says)   mysterious

                         y   l   o

it the
proper of
I've without
shadow planned
no the
the in
powder was
(shall get
clean machine
blade the
soap proper
trying I
here edge-on
the and
but for
on anyway
get I
a make
just more
full me
its enough
bar cleaner?
in some
the this

course there's
there opportunity
the equipment
was job
a is
a myself
water to
the was
done ransack
for shadow
the bath
job me
to shadow
word cannot
to sideways
or could
say) business
of go
like course
to like
use know
I because
going that
would about

there's course
opportunity there
equipment the
job was
is a
myself a
to water
was the
ransack done
shadow for
bath the
me job
shadow to
cannot word
sideways to
could or
business say)
go of
course like
like to
know use
because I
that going
about would

the it
of proper
without I've
planned shadow
the no
in the
was powder
get (shall
machine clean
the blade
proper soap
I trying
edge-on here
and the
for but
anyway on
I get
make a
more just
me full
enough its
cleaner? bar
some in
this the

sun   green   trees   *hiding*
indelible   *her school*
no to every day   *tunnel*
hot water   *veil*
spring attire just above grass
coffee travels through air
wires   *banter from him*
sheep   *containers*
I will not say a word
swallow   *he's happy*   *yellow*
look at that field   *copse*
growing up   yellow line
keep back   shadow moves
not so yellow from this angle
this pen shows through
noetry   turn up   *back light*
milk used up   *some degree*
sun in my eyes   *a wok of seafood*
new manager under table
ring ring   cut   *accurate*
beans chance   *pool of yellow*
I will not say
each layer greyer
copper feather   *glass memory*
line too wide   *chocolate ten*
tumulus it isn't   *a grey idea*
a grey sentence   *let it be misunderstood*
in darkness   *may add lapel*
caravans   *narrowboats*
snap stirrer   *write across shading*
it is always write   *available*   the long dark
near the bombings they still have their hair cut
and prepare red carcasses
alarm   *dots*   sun still
that's upholstery canvas   oh you call it scrim
buttercups   posts
why have they discontinued pilot?
she will bristle   *will dry slowly*
1950s concrete design   *biffa*
bleeds from brickwork (white)
a scramble   a scribble   *yet*
a few stand among the red and white columns
why capitals there?

56

like this, like that
blah blah like a blah blah
deny simile

they they to black
were see consciousness) in
I it the bag
(plastic) know know some
descend fact have with
I one something the
bald headed when kite
a don't painted as
any chewed kite the
a blue I noticed
the stairs be our
of feet on of
I may be that
ladybirds by the at
to by not cork
the real some were
all (but kind into
a red in with
containing point those red
painted socks hell I
and although paper the
of horse tiled still
which drawings I plastic
rehearsals took even from
dog it though (there
floor see deeper another
but that deeper home
a all am and
the provided prevailed a
bed horse of one
thought for blue I
time the to more
brown the blue me
turquoise in food leads
there a as but
down as a girls
extraordinary I it taking
and lumbering the photographer
kite) the disturbed thought
didn't of was and
only feet the pictures
came (what so on

The piping starts early
cutting the dark in half

                    I thought it would be absent this year,
                    but no, it was there again

along with the gibbon
born from the plane tree limbs   still there a decade later.

Forest years, diminished chords,
forgotten quavers, abandoned inspiration.

                    I expected the song to die.
                    Surprise can surprise. Otters

risk everything in the muddy water.
Overwhelmed, I view the jaguar

                              crushing a caiman's skull.

Tree roots tangle in Brazil;
branches scramble in London.

sunspots notwithstanding (
and he says that he never
uses 'beforehand') those
leaf green vermiculations
are the (what?) the water
not the hot god.
if a rider and his charge
were taken for a single being
(going off on one, Picasso) then
they cannot be blamed
for getting it wrong and fleeing
instantaneously. blimey!
those lionised scrawlers keep
doing it, keep tearing off
my milky cataracts.
from their smug shores of rectitude
they raise the green dragon.
but I can be the gull, given
the blue, clear air unnetted.
I can stumble upon pathways
to the laughing sea, a
cantilevered forest or hold
a match to waxed beret wicks.
when I am a boulder,
the gull will show me
how to breathe.

The sea climbs up the sky –
flat grey; grey and flat.

His pen writes about his hand,
nothing more; obvious yet crystal.

His hand rests on the open book;
wrinkled light reveals the devil.

The journey from his eye
to the pencil's echo is unimpeded.

And the sea rolls and rocks
on its heels, healing his eyes.

But the sea is not blameless. Its
retreat is a possibility.

Turn the jacket, lining outward.
Opalescent; inside pocket names the hoodwinked one.

Oak bark swallowed by its tree –
first ring surfaces, peepers blinking.

'Hugger mugger', she said, the meaning wrong.
Walk-outs threatened. Someone was chosen.

Voices wrap the evening
and the long-haired privet laughs.

black sun rises up one end　　medieval grille　　mausoleum
smooth wood blocks　　my father drew the hand that painted the
coming of day　　and the lady sits reading　　a snake was under the
written stone　　and in the dark place the lines undulate　　voices
against voice　　looks out from curls of ink　　the soul breathes in the
voice of a believer　　the point was touched　　I make bags with
holes　　you're offset　　the soul is behind the box　　the woods
people look behind the box　　sort of toy crowns for giants　　these
flags don't flap in the wind　　Narcissus looks at Korea　　could be a
wind sock　　basin　　drone　　not a Scottish air but a thing about a
mistaken heartache　　while you look at blue and yellow snow voices
return　　roll round in a hamster's wheel　　an unfinished what?
ffour vvoice bboxes　　rolled up voices　　the camera goes round and I
see I am a man　　we saw them in Scotland on their lek　　frayed
hairstyles without a clutch of turquoise eggs　　dragonfly's wings cut
twice

... ardour ... ardour ...... ardour ...
... ardour ... ardour .... ardour ...
ardour .... ardent .... ardour .... ardour
... ardent .... ardour ..... ardour .....
... ardour ..... ardour .... ardour ...
... ardour .... ardour .... ardour ..
... ardour ..... ardour .... ardour ...
... ardour .... ardour .... ardour ...
ardour .... ardent .... ardour .... ardour
... ardent .... ardour ..... ardour ......

l'

m

John washed his body from head to coccyx when he awoke on the first day of his sojourn in Gibraltar. It was demanded that he be odourless for the task he was to perform. His orders were plain – he should search the shoreline for shells bearing a text in miniature handwriting on their inner surfaces. The script would be indecipherable to John; it was necessary only that he should find the shells. When seven prime examples had been gathered, he should return to the base with them, wrapped carefully in seaweed. His commander would reward him with a kiss.   c

{Just take the word 'yellow' and add water}

The old masters had only the very poisonous   a
orpiment, yellow sulphide of arsenic, and realgar, arsenic
orange (arsenic disulphide), to work with. It was
very coarsely ground and applied with tempera. In
oil painting it was used pure without admixtures
between layers of varnish. In Pompeii it has
frequently been discovered in ochres, but it has
also been traced in present-day cadmiums.

|

risotto rice
bread
salad
washing up liquid
washing powder
Guardian
oranges
onions
lavatory cleaner
tuna |
blackmail

n

A few popes

St. Linus: 67–76
St. Hyginus: 136–140
St. Soter: 166–175
St. Eutychian: 275–283
St. Hilarius: 461–468
St. Hormisdas: 514–523
Boniface II: 530–532

i

g

There was a time when we boys
ran round the field for 'chocolate'.
Quick runners had none; they
always laughed at the lack.

Would the great traveller, St. X.,
have swung the stick at the end
of the race if he'd been there?

Are you asking me to sprinkle lime
in his coffin; pinch his left leg; shave
his ever-fruitful beard?

His blood still flowed three months
later, but before that he'd rolled up
his sleeves and cured the plague.
Such stories are gospel in Goa.

f

A few kings

Egbert: 827–830
Ethelwulf: 839–857
Ethelbald: 857–860
Ethelbert: 860–866
Ethelred: 866–871
Alfred the Great: 871–899
Edward the Elder: 899–925

The moorland exhaled a fresh mauve breath as the summer dawn rose. On the horizon, a figure became visible, striding purposefully in my direction. Although several hundred yards off, I guessed it to be a man. The chill mist, which clung here and there to the bracken, occasionally enveloped him. As he advanced, he swiped restlessly at the vegetation with his stick, and I wondered whether I would know him when our paths crossed.

Momentarily, I became distracted by a loose lace on one of my walking boots and stooped to tie it up. When I resumed an upright position the walker had evaporated, as though swallowed whole by some vaporous hell-hound.

Why had Frank Boscombe's name muscled into my consciousness? He'd been a friend from my days on the island, with whom I'd lost contact. But I knew him to be dead. A cold ripple ran up my legs as I ....

The very shadows assumed the colours of their mothers.
The very shadows assumed the colours of their mothers.
The very shadows assumed the colours of their mothers.
The very shadows assumed the colours of their mothers.
The very shadows assumed the colours of their mothers.
The very shadows assumed the colours of their mothers.
The very shadows assumed the colours of their mothers.
The very shadows assumed the colours of their mothers.
The very shadows assumed the colours of their mothers.
The very shadows assumed the colours of their mothers.

Describing the nutritional requirements for the weekend fishing trip when he returned, Michel surprised everybody, even his ageing mother, by divulging the extraordinary patterns of thought expounded by the rest of the group when questions were put to them challenging their outlook on piscatorial death. ʊ

He was known as an awkward man,   Contrary to popular opinion,
The Painter; even his daughter told us so.   the farmer rose from his bed
(You are not needed; don't expect smiles).   at five o'clock in the morning.
While the world celebrates D-Day   He was a man of routine and could not rest
he languishes where someone has placed   until he had counted every last one
him, behind the sink's knobbled tap.   of his decorated porcelain eggs.

G

There, he dreams himself in cadmium red; in bed   His was the only comprehensive set
as usual, smoking as usual, naked bulb burning. If   of Calitrant de Mercy's stupendous
piled boots were part of his dream and the plate   inventions. The farmer kept
of biscuits a snack for now, nobody would know.   the de Mercy collection secreted
All that can be said is that they are there, and   in the depths of his cellar. Each egg was
his midnight story re-told at the corner of time.   elaborately documented in a

o

She sailed this side
of the ancient stone wall,

tacking back and forth
in her fibreglass dinghy.

There were no thoughts
for the walled-up country

of her own ignorance.
Over that ivy-festooned barrier

e

scurrilous mumblings failed
to reach her muffled ears, 'She

doesn't know of red romans,
those hairy, ten-legged creatures.'

The bursting rooms of velvet
obliquely held their tongues.

r

g

It was on one such occasion that Bernard Turnstope began his consideration of Ignorance. A shift in his outlook had brought him to the realisation that it was an unusually variable and absorbing subject. He surmised, 'All people are incapable of knowing everything, and ignorance is only the deficit of knowledge.'

e.   A vast tract of cerebral countryside was opened for Bernard as he began to compare himself to Leonardo da Vinci, Sappho, the stocktaker at Tesco's and the oldest man in the world, Dmitri Sholakovsky. 'All their knowledges are different but their ignorance is the same! In that respect, I must be Albert Einstein's equal.'

Credits

A Chameleon in the Valley, 2003. First published to accompany the exhibition, *Infallible, In Search of the Real George Eliot*, ARTicle Press, 2003. By kind permission of Roxy Walsh. The section, 'The old masters had ...' is quoted from Max Doerner, *The Materials of the Artist*, trans. Eugen Neuhaus, Rupert Hart-Davis Ltd, London, 1969, pp.65–66.

All the barbers are brothers, 2013

amalgam, 2010. First published in Fabian Peake, *Amalgam, Collection of Poems and Writings 2000-2010*, UBU editions: Publishing the Unpublishable, edited and with kind permission of Kenneth Goldsmith.

approximate (2), 2010. First published in Fabian Peake, *Amalgam, Collection of Poems and Writings 2000-2010*, UBU editions: Publishing the Unpublishable, edited and with kind permission of Kenneth Goldsmith.

Away in Texas, 2003. First published in *Abridged 0-22: Nostalgia is a Loaded Gun*, 2011. By kind permission of Gregory McCartney.

Black winds, 2013

Eye, 2012

fox (auto-da-fé), 2013

frigate, 1999

Fruits, 1997

Fungi, 1996. First published to accompany an exhibition at Kukje Gallery, Seoul, South Korea, 2012. By kind permission of Eemyun Kang.

Hampstead Heath, 1996

he walks the horizontal ladder, 2011

hiatus, 2001

it the course there's, 2011

it took time for the green, 2011

Loose Monk, 2003

mistake, 2012

Not as if, 1998

Our Hedge, 1996. First published in Fabian Peake, *Through a Window*, Manchester Metropolitan University, 1996.

song thrush, 2007

stretch, 1999

stretched out over many miles, 2010

sun green trees hiding, 2006

Sunrise, 1998

sunspots notwithstanding (, 2011

that light, the light of five, 2009

The bucket I hold, 2014

The Letter, 1997. First published in the compendium for the Prinzhorn Collection, Heidelberg, Germany, 2013. By kind permission of Ingrid von Beyme.

The Looter, 1998
The piping starts early, 2014
The sea climbs up the sky, 2014
The Search, 1998
The women look, 2013. First published in */seconds. 14*, online magazine.
By kind permission of Peter Lewis.
they talk about colours, 2009
they they to black, 2011
this alley a brick wall, 2011
two step, 2000
unknown, 2001
woodcock, 2008
yet, 2001

Acknowledgements

I would like to thank my wife Phyllida and our children Florence, Clover, Tabitha, Eddie and Lewis for all their encouragement regarding the book. I would also like to thank my parents, Mervyn Peake and Maeve Gilmore who, during their lifetime gave me such unconditional support in my work as an artist and writer, and thanks to my sister Clare Peñate and my late brother, Sebastian, who was so loyal in his enthusiasm for my work.

I would, of course, like to thank Jeremy Akerman, Eileen Daly and Mali Clements for their enormous help during the making of the book.

Akerman Daly sincerely thank everyone who so generously supported the book at the outset. Their commitment made the book possible. Thank you Sean and Julia Windett, Matthew Windett, Kyra Mathers, Katy Windett, James Windett, Eemyun Kang, Mali Morris and Stephen Lewis, Marjorie Allthorpe-Guyton, Luke and Jane Mitcheson, Daniel Lancaster, Katrin Mäurich, Crescent Arts, Ingrid Swenson and Andrew Wilson, Alex Wilson, Miranda Glossop, Penelope Treadwell, Fiona Banner, Marcella and Gavin Menzies, Ros Odling-Smee, Camilla and Anthony Whitworth-Jones, Richard Salmon, Christopher Phillips and Manou Shama-Levy, Anthony and Ann Hill, Nicky Harlow, Stephanie Seungmin Kim, Mr O. J. A. Gilmore, Jess Flood-Paddock, Malcolm Craddock, Vanessa Jackson, Pamela Golden, Julia Swann, Tina Reid, Louis Hartnoll, Ben Hillwood-Harris, Annelies Oberdanner, Christina Mackie, Jes Fernie, Tony Grisoni and Oona Grimes, Jane Rolo, Anne Elizabeth Mills, Lucy Moore, Derek Wilson, Alison Clements, Kathy Luff, Carl Freedman, Teresa Grimes, Darren Bender, Gina Medcalf, Tamsin Clark, Ruth Kitching, Matthew Shaul, Mat Jenner, Book Works, Anne Odling-Smee, Ciprian Muraru, William Palin, Tamarin Norwood, Diego Ferrari, Steven J. Fowler, Andrew Hunt, Tiffany Jenkins, Jay Jopling, Daniela Cascella, Justin Oh, Patrick Coyle and Stef Hirsch, Simon Goudie, Elena Crippa, Doro Globus, Sharon Morris, Jo Stockham, Karen Knorr, Literary Kitchen, Niamh de Valera, and those who wish to remain anonymous.

Akerman Daly would also like to thank the Peake family, Karsten Schubert, Doro Globus, Louisa Green, Daniel Griffiths, Mat Jenner and Arts Council England, Fraser Muggeridge, Carol Montpart and Alex Kerr for their help in making the book. We especially thank Fabian.

Loose Monk
Poems by Fabian Peake

Published in 2014 by Akerman Daly

Akerman Daly
6 Victoria Chambers
Luke Street
London EC2A 4EE
United Kingdom
akermandaly.com

In association with
Ridinghouse
46 Lexington Street
London W1F 0LP
United Kingdom
ridinghouse.co.uk

Distributed in the UK
and Europe by
Cornerhouse
70 Oxford Street
Manchester M1 5NG
United Kingdom
cornerhouse.org

Distributed in the US by
RAM Publications + Distribution, Inc.
2525 Michigan Avenue Building A2
Santa Monica, CA, 90404
United States
rampub.com

Hardback edition
ISBN 978 0 9930181 0 7
Softcover Akerman Daly
ISBN 978 0 9930181 1 4
Softcover Ridinghouse
ISBN 978 1 909932 00 5

Edited by Jeremy Akerman
and Eileen Daly
Publishing assistance by Mali Clements
Design by Fraser Muggeridge studio
Printed in Belgium by Cassochrome